# TENNYSON

# TENNYSON

## THE LESLIE STEPHEN LECTURE

DELIVERED IN THE SENATE HOUSE, CAMBRIDGE
ON 11 NOVEMBER 1909

BY

## WILLIAM PATON KER, M.A.

ALL SOULS COLLEGE, OXFORD

Cambridge :
at the University Press
1909

# CAMBRIDGE
## UNIVERSITY PRESS

University Printing House, Cambridge CB2 8BS, United Kingdom

Published in the United States of America by Cambridge University Press, New York

Cambridge University Press is part of the University of Cambridge.

It furthers the University's mission by disseminating knowledge in the pursuit of
education, learning and research at the highest international levels of excellence.

www.cambridge.org
Information on this title: www.cambridge.org/9781107679955

First published 1909
First paperback edition 2014

*A catalogue record for this publication is available from the British Library*

ISBN 978-1-107-67995-5 Paperback

# TENNYSON

An invitation to give this lecture before the University of Cambridge is an honour too great for any conventional words of acknowledgment; but I may be permitted at the outset to offer my thanks to the University, and further to say that even if it had been possible to decline an invitation which comes with more than the force of a command, the name of Leslie Stephen would have been enough to drive away all craven scruples, and to put spirit, as he has done so often, into the hesitating wits and will.

No one standing in this place with a task so serious before him could ask for better auspices; and I think it a fortunate thing that I am able to remember Leslie Stephen here to-day as in a sort of way his vassal and one of his company. I have sat by his side at College tables; I heard him speak, in

December 1894, his noble commemoration of Stevenson, and although unhappily he had given up his occupation as Chief Guide before I was sworn in as one of the Sunday Tramps, yet my name is there in the list, and it will be a pleasure, I hope, to one or two others, as it is to myself, to find that one of the Sunday Tramps, though the latest and the least worthy, has been asked to give this lecture. But apart from these personal and private matters—which still I am bold to think are not irrelevant nor unworthy of this audience— the name of Stephen brings with it the thought of everything that is honest and sincere; it gives the best encouragement that anyone could wish, though it does not make the task, in itself, less difficult.

In the Lives of the Poets, as of other men, we have all our favourite passages to which we turn by preference, and which we make into symbols or examples, standing for all the rest; or which perhaps we remember for some trivial reason or unreason, because they touch on some associations of our own. Out

of the Life of Tennyson I take one thing
which is not altogether trifling, and which
seems to me to be characteristic and memor-
able, though it is not part of the common
tradition, the things that are generally re-
peated about the poet. It is the misunder-
standing between himself and his friend
Monckton Milnes over the poem which
Tennyson refused at first to send to the al-
bum—*The Tribute*—which Milnes was editing.

Milnes was offended and wrote an angry
letter. Tennyson's reply (given in the two
biographies, Lord Houghton's and his own)
brings out the character, temper and humour
of a very remarkable man dealing with a very
severe trial of his patience. His friend had
lost his head, but kept his talent for language,
and in some of his carefully chosen phrases
(like 'piscatory vanity') had shown that he
meant not only to quarrel but to wound.
Tennyson's answer is a proof of the virtue of
imagination in dealing with practical affairs.
Milnes's sharpened phrases have their full
effect, and Tennyson suffers the pain that

was intended. Anger comes also, not mere resentment, but the passion that would have destroyed all vestiges of friendship. That can be made out from Tennyson's words: 'I put down my pipe and stared at the fire for ten minutes till the stranger vanished up the chimney.'

Milnes, the smaller man, had been only able to think of one thing; his friend in those ten minutes staring at the fire had taken in the case in all its bearings; had felt the injury, had understood the irritation of his friend, and been bitterly amused by his vanity and dumbfounded by his want of sense. Staring at the fire, he had seen all this as a poor wretched thing which *the Stranger*, the Accuser, was doing his worst to make into a lasting enmity. He stares the stranger out of countenance and up the chimney; the friendship remains unbroken, because Tennyson is magnanimous; and one need not require any more convincing proof of the largeness and generosity of his nature and his mind; of his intellectual virtue, if I may use the term freely and in no restricted or scholastic sense.

For many years past the Devil's Advocate has been busy, and it is impossible to ignore him. It is not on the ground of the biography but on the poems themselves that he must be met; nevertheless I take this passage from the biography to begin with, to show what sort of a man Tennyson might be in a problem and ordeal of personal conduct. The Lives of the Poets are often useful to correct false impressions; the Lives of Wordsworth and Keats do not prove that they were good poets, but they show that their adversaries were mistaken about them. Wordsworth among the Girondists, taking a share in the French Revolution, and Keats on his long walking-tour, travelling to the Ross of Mull, are very different from the tame soft creatures which some of their reviewers imagined them to be. Tennyson's character was often misjudged in a similar way; the Life of Tennyson makes it impossible to repeat the old false opinions.

The Devil's Advocate is always worth listening to, and not always easy to refute. It may be true that Homer could not draw the maps of a campaign nor the plan of a country-house; that Dante was too reckless in his punishments and too careful about the spots in the moon; that Milton went wrong, if not as Bentley thought yet in the way Pope has described him. It is easy to collect instances of this kind, and of a much severer kind, about these and other great poets. But the plain man (though his authority would hardly be allowed either by Milton or Tennyson) is generally right, even if he may not be right in all particulars as to this sort of argument. The plain man feels simply that the good things are not touched; that even though the faults and errors may detract from one's estimate of the poet's work as a whole, they do not spoil the good things. Let us suppose that the *Lady of Shalott* and the *Lotos Eaters* and *Tithonus* are absolutely good; then they are not less good because other less good things were written by the author of them. The plain man looks to those peaks and summits of poetry and finds them beyond all comparison with the lower levels where the historical critic is working out his survey. The critic will go wrong unless he recognises this other point of view and the fact that a good poem has a value of its own which nothing can spoil, as nothing in the world can take the place of it. The essence of a poem is that it should be remembered for what it is, not that it should be catalogued in an historical series in relation with what it is not. This is not meant to depreciate criticism or the history of literature, but to show their necessary limitations; which perhaps are sufficiently obvious.

It is not enough for a poem that it should be what is called 'touching'; one remembers Goethe's deadly saying about the hearts of sensibility: 'any bungler can touch them.' But it remains true that if a poem is not wonderful it is nothing; here as in philosophy wonder is the beginning of wisdom, and the end too, when the wonder of novelty has turned into the deeper wonder at the well-known, the familiar, the unfathomable beauty.

Where did the new music of Tennyson come from? It is the sort of question that the critic is always asking, and it is not as foolish as it looks. It is true that a good poem is a singular and miraculous thing; it is also true that most good poems have ancestors. Here we come to the other side of the matter. The plain man is justified in saying, as against the critic, that the *Lady of Shalott* and the *Lotos Eaters* are not spoilt by anything the critic may have to say about other things. But he is not justified if he says that the critic has no business to meddle with the ancestry of these poems; that it is irrelevant to look for the old story of Shalott, and impertinent to compare the *Lotos Eaters* with *The Castle of Indolence*. Here the weakness of the plain man is apt to show itself. He thinks too idolatrously of what he worships; he thinks that the more you know about the poem the less you will admire it. It may be so sometimes, but the poem that is damaged in this way is not worth troubling about. The Commentator of course needs to be carefully watched. He must not here debate the question whether Astolat is Guildford, as Malory says, or Dumbarton, as another author has surmised. But he will gain something if he follows out Mr Palgrave's note to the *Golden Treasury* and finds the old Italian story in the *Cento novelle antiche*, which was read by Tennyson and from which he took the matter of his poem. This original story is not the same thing as Malory. It is taken from the same source as Malory, 'the French book' of *Lancelot*. But it has quite a different effect, and the effect is nearly related to the English poem. The Italian story, like the English poem, is detached from its context; it is not like the Idyll of *Elaine*, part of a large and complicated history. The Italian story has no ties and dependencies; it is a thing by itself, in the old clear language, one of the beautiful small things of medieval art. It does not trouble itself with the story of the maid of Astolat as it is given in detail in the French book and in Malory; it takes hardly anything from the French book but the death of the Lady of Shalott; the voyage in the boat without a steersman; and the marvel in the Court of King Arthur at Camelot.

Great part of the beauty of Tennyson's poem comes from the mystery of its story. It is a lyrical romance, and its setting is in a visionary land; there is no burden of historical substance in it as there is in the *Idylls of the King*. This strange isolation of the story, making its own world, is part of the old Italian *novella*; and it is this quality which makes the greatest distinction in the new order of romantic poetry to which Tennyson's poem belongs. It is this which is found in *La Belle Dame sans Mercy* and in the most magical poems of William Morris's first volume. It makes these poems, and *The Lady of Shalott* along with them, very different from the older romantic school

which went often to the Middle Ages for
material, but (generally speaking) was rather
dull regarding the medieval form. Neither
*La Belle Dame sans Mercy* nor *The Lady of
Shalott* nor *Golden Wings* is a close imitation
of medieval art; but they all have that
strange homeless quality which is found in
some of the finest (not the most ambitious)
medieval poems.

The verse of a poet shows his poetical
ancestry better than anything else. Every-
where in the older poets one comes on the
elements of Tennyson's verse. He knew all
the different modes, from the least regular
to the most exact. Coleridge's complaint (as
recorded in his *Table Talk*, April 24, 1833)
that Mr Tennyson ' has begun to write verses
without very well understanding what metre
is ' is partly explained by the many poems in
irregular verse in the early volumes. But
these volumes show also—and show in per-
fection—Tennyson's command of the familiar
forms and his skill in using them. In the
verse of *Mariana* there is no technical in-

novation; only the common elementary forms
are employed in a new way :—

> With blackest moss the flower-plots
>   Were thickly crusted, one and all:
> The rusted nails fell from the knots
>   That held the peach to the garden-wall.
> The broken sheds looked sad and strange;
>   Unlifted was the clinking latch ;
>   Weeded and worn the ancient thatch;
> Upon the lonely moated grange.

For one thing, the short line is here made
weighty and solemn, nearly the equal of the
heroic line.   This in itself is no new effect,
but it is used here in a new pattern; and the
change from the alternate rhymes of the first
quatrain to the *In Memoriam* stanza in the
second is poetical invention.

There are two great families of verse (not
two only) in modern poetry, which can be
traced back to the beginnings of modern
poetry in Provence about the year 1100.   One
is used for long-sustained passages, and the
heroic line is its chief instrument, as in the
*Faerie Queene* or in *Paradise Lost* : the other
has a shorter length of wave and rings more

clearly; its base is generally the octosyllable. The poets may sometimes be divided into the one class or the other; thus Spenser, with the great Italian poets, belongs almost entirely to the first order; Burns, with Villon, to the second. Tennyson is of both parties; he uses the fuller measure, the larger period, in *The Lotos Eaters*, not to speak of his blank verse; but *In Memoriam* is in the shorter line, and from the first, from the 'Chorus in an unpublished drama written early,' he used the shorter line in its full strength:—

> Each sun which from the centre flings
> > Grand music and redundant fire,
> The burning belts, the mighty rings,
> > The murmurous planets' rolling choir.

Gray had the same equal skill in both kinds. The Pindaric odes belong to the first; while for the second we may quote *The Long Story*:—

> Full oft within the spatious walls,
> > When he had fifty winters o'er him,
> My grave Lord-Keeper led the brawls;
> > The seals and maces danc'd before him.

Which might easily be taken for Tennyson's own.

Burns's verse was imitated by Tennyson, as it had been by Praed, and it is possible to find in Burns some lines that agree, not only in metre, but in mode of speech, in poetic energy, in resonant phrase, with the manner of Tennyson. I mean particularly the motto of *The Holy Fair* ('Hypocrisy *à la mode*'):—

> A robe of seeming truth and trust
>   Hid crafty observation,
> And secret hung with poison'd crust
>   The dirk of defamation;
> A mask that like the gorget show'd
>   Dye-varying on the pigeon,
> While for a mantle large and broad
>   He wrapt him in religion.

Tennyson uses this form in *Will Water-proof* and *Amphion*, and fills it in the same way with compressed significant language; making, in *Will Waterproof*, a small technical change (feminine rhyme in the second qua-train only), but otherwise keeping the old measure. There is no better example than the stanza into which he has put Will Waterproof's vision of the whole world, the

verses where the ancient quarrel between
philosophy and poetry seems to be recon-
ciled by the influence of the Muse and the
help of her Lusitanian servant:—

> This earth is rich in man and maid;
>     With fair horizons bound:
> This whole wide earth of light and shade
>     Comes out a perfect round.
> High over roaring Temple-bar,
>     And set in Heaven's third story,
> I look at all things as they are,
>     But thro' a kind of glory.

The new varieties of rhyme invented for
*The Daisy* and the poem addressed *to
F. D. Maurice* are among the most de-
lightful things of this sort in the language,
and the beauty of Tennyson's art would suffer
wrong if these were not remembered:—

> I climb'd the roofs at break of day,
> Sun-smitten Alps before me lay;
>     I stood among the silent statues
> And statued pinnacles, mute as they.

> How faintly-flush'd, how phantom-fair,
> Was Monte Rosa, hanging there
>     A thousand shadowy-pencill'd valleys
> And snowy dells in a golden air.

In these and in a host of other rhymes Tennyson has done what Sidney has given as the work of the poet: 'to make the too much loved earth more lovely.' They dwell in the memory, like

> The rich Virgilian rustic measure
> Of Lari Maxume, all the way.

Tennyson's blank verse is of many different kinds, almost as various as Wordsworth's. Here again it is possible to find anticipations, in older poets, of some of Tennyson's effects; in Landor's *Gebir* for example:—

> And the long moonbeam on the hard wet sand
> Lay like a jasper column half upreared.

What strikes one first, and at first with pleasure, is the ingenuity of Tennyson's variations. He uses his blank verse according to Pope's rules in the *Essay on Criticism*; he is fond of rendering Ajax and Camilla in the movement of his line. This is Ajax:—

> He felt were she the prize of bodily force
> Himself beyond the rest pushing could move
> The chair of Idris.

This is Camilla, a little retarded :—

> But while the sun yet beat a dewy blade
> The sound of many a heavily galloping hoof
> Smote on her ear, and turning round she saw
> Dust, and the points of lances bicker in it.

These passages are both taken from *Enid*, and there are many more in the same Idyll. There may be too much of this device; yet it cannot be fairly said that these conceits of verse break up the solidity of the poem. Many different motives and graces are combined in the Idyll :—

> as one
> That listens near a torrent mountain brook
> All through the crash of the near cataract hears
> The drumming thunder of the huger fall.

The likeness of Tennyson to Pope in some things is undeniable. There is the same clearness, the same regard for elegance of verse. Even in the noting of particulars, though Pope is not near Tennyson in fineness of perception, and though the fashion of his age discouraged such things, there are some resemblances. We all know the result of Tennyson's poetry in *Cranford*:—'This young man comes and tells me that ash buds are black; and I look, and they *are* black.' In like manner many people who had played cards all their lives must have read the *Rape of the Lock* and been told for the first time by that other young poet that the King of Diamonds is always seen in profile, and must have looked and verified the statement that the only King who carries the globe is the King of Clubs. Tennyson's *Princess* is full of things that make it a modern counterpart to the *Rape of the Lock*. A poet's quality may be proved in his least substantial work, and this that follows is Tennyson's poetry, not at its highest, but no less authentic than the highest:—

> —and then we turn'd, we wound
> About the cliffs, the copses, out and in,
> Hammering and clinking, chattering stony names
> Of shale and hornblende, rag and trap and tuff,
> Amygdaloid and trachyte, till the sun
> Grew broader toward his death and fell, and all
> The rosy heights came out above the lawns.

Blank verse can do anything; among other things it may be lyrical. Wordsworth knew this when he put a note to *Tintern Abbey* to say that he would not call it an Ode, which means, of course, that he had thought of it as an Ode and wished it to be so thought of. *Oenone* is a lyrical poem following the example of the Greek Idylls with their lyrical refrain; but the chief poem of this kind is *Tithonus,* which has no refrain, and so escapes from the touch of artificiality which might possibly be charged against the imitation of Theocritus. And in *Tithonus* there are none of those curiosities of verse, those 'Ajax' and 'Camilla' passages, which are so common in the *Idylls of the King.* The verse is all of the pure classical tradition—there are no variations beyond what are commonly recognised and known to every beginner. Yet the life in the poem is infinite and infinitely varied:—

Whispering I knew not what of wild and sweet
Like that strange song I heard Apollo sing
While Ilion like a mist rose into towers.

2—2

The Devil's Advocate is very ready to discuss Tennyson's 'thought.' An instance is given by Mr Gladstone in his essay on *Locksley Hall* (*Nineteenth Century*, January 1887). He quotes an article 'of singular talent' in the *Pall Mall Gazette*, December 14, 1886. This 'states rather dogmatically that any criticism which accepts Lord Tennyson as a thinker is out of date,' and Mr Gladstone proceeds: 'I venture to demur to this proposition and to contend that the author of *In Memoriam* (for example) shows a capacity which entitles him to a high place among the thinkers of the day.'

Now it may be asked whether this demurrer does not concede too much to the Devil's Advocate of the *Pall Mall Gazette.* 'Thinker' is taken as if it were a simple unequivocal term. What it meant exactly as used by those two parties would be hard to say; but the Index to that volume of the *Nineteenth Century*, which contains articles by Professor Huxley, Mr John Morley and

the Duke of Argyll, suggests some of the
names, 'the thinkers of the day,' with whom
Tennyson is to be ranked or not to be ranked,
according to one or the other opinion.
Thought is here discursive thought, philo-
sophical or moral argument. Tennyson as a
thinker is compared with thinkers who use
prose. There need not be any unfairness in
this. There certainly are poems, like the
*Essay on Man*, which enter into competition
with the prose thinkers, and whose arguments
are fairly judged by the same standards.
There is nothing unfair that I can see in
Mr Gladstone's discussion of *Locksley Hall*.
Whether his arguments are really valid is
another question. Is the contention of
*Locksley Hall sixty years after* really met
by Mr Gladstone's references to the penny
post, cheap newspapers, and Mr Thomas
Cook's tourist agency? It may be doubted.
A Canadian critic at the time (with perhaps
a little too much emphasis) said it was
almost as if someone had answered John
the Baptist 'by pointing out that there had

been great improvements in the Roman Law, that the system of imperial roads had been successfully developed, that the harbour accommodation at Ravenna had been increased, and that there had been a gratifying activity during a recent period in the building trade at Caesarea Philippi.' But however that may be, there can be no doubt of Mr Gladstone's good faith in the argument, nor of his right to take it up. Both the earlier and the later *Locksley Hall* are full of debatable matter. Both are criticisms of life, and what is criticism if it may not be challenged and canvassed?

But there are other kinds of poetic thought besides that which can be discussed in prose. The poets, like other men, can play with all sorts of debatable commonplaces, and sometimes it is pleasant enough to follow them, to trace for instance Shakespeare on the human will and destiny, 'the fated sky,' 'the inward quality,'—to compare the reflections of Hamlet or Brutus with the dogmatic certainty of Lysander, waking up under the

spell of Puck and Oberon, and beginning
at once:—

> The will of man is by his reason sway'd.

But the poetical mode of thought is not
shown best in the poet's moralising sentences.
The noblest poetic thought has often very
little that can be debated.  The poetic discourse of *Obermann* cannot hold its own, for
poetic wisdom, against the conclusion of
*Sohrab and Rustum*, and if we were to
choose, in Mr Arnold's own way, a passage
of deep seriousness from his books, it might
well be *Cadmus and Harmonia* rather than
the song of Empedocles.

> And there they say two bright and aged snakes
> Who once were Cadmus and Harmonia
> Bask in the glens or on the warm sea-shore
> In breathless quiet, after all their ills;
> Nor do they see their country, nor the place
> Where the Sphinx lived among the frowning hills,
> Nor the unhappy palace of their race,
> Nor Thebes, nor the Ismenus any more.

Two of the most solemn passages in all
poetry are the argument of true Fame in

*Lycidas* and the speech over the death of
Samson:—

Nothing is here for tears, nothing to wail
Or knock the breast; no weakness, no contempt,
Dispraise or blame, nothing but well and fair,
With what may quiet us in a death so noble.

These meditations of the poet are wronged
if any word is said about them in discussion
of their substance; one may argue with
Milton about 'the ruin of our corrupted
clergy then at their height,' but not about
his poetical doctrine of true Fame:—

That strain we heard was of a higher mood.

So we may hold that the thought of
Tennyson is not so well bestowed in the
argumentative poems (like that which Mr
Gladstone refuted in the *Nineteenth Century*)
as in some of those where he uses mythology,
the legends of *Tithonus* or the *Holy Grail,*
to convey his reading of the world. The
difference between the two kinds of thought
is very great; and the nobler kind is not
discourse but vision. It does not lend itself

to discussion; if it is once apprehended there is no more to be said, or no more than the words of Sir Bors in the *Holy Grail*:—

> Ask me not, for I may not speak of it,
> I saw it.

One need not be afraid to defend the 'thought' of Tennyson on the lower ground either. But there is not much to be gained for his poetry in this way. Much of his reasoning is opinion, as good as that of other thinkers, but not founded as most of Wordsworth's is on certain and irrefragable knowledge. It is generally far above the range of ordinary didactic poetry, but much of it has suffered through lapse of time and the change of fashions, and has become antiquated like the *Essay on Man*. What least injured in this way, what best retains its value as philosophy, is the poem of the *Ancient Sage*, which is based on experience like that of Wordsworth's; and the wisdom of the *Ancient Sage* is summed up in the sentence that 'nothing worthy proving can

be proven.' Noble as this is, one feels that
it is less excellent than the mythological
poems, where the thought is inextricable
from the bodily form, as in *Tithonus*:—

Upon thy glimmering thresholds, when the steam
Floats up from those dim fields about the homes
Of happy men that have the power to die,
And grassy barrows of the happier dead.
Release me, and restore me to the ground;
Thou seest all things, thou wilt see my grave:
Thou wilt renew thy beauty morn by morn;
I earth in earth forget these empty courts,
And thee returning on thy silver wheels.

It is contended by some of the critics,
and among them by some of the greatest
admirers of Tennyson's poetry, that he in-
dulges his genius too much in curiosities
of detail, in decorations that break the
structure. Besides the turns of his verse,
there are devices of fancy, it is said, which
are too minute and exquisite for great poetry.
The illustrations are too much for the main
fabric. Certainly Tennyson makes a liberal
use of the Homeric simile; and the Homeric

simile, no doubt, may be overdone. It has often been satirised in many mock heroic works. But it survives; it is one of the great beauties of *Hyperion*; there is as much of it in *Sohrab and Rustum* as in the *Idylls of the King*, and in neither is it untrue to its origin :—

So the sweet voice of Enid moved Geraint ;
And made him like a man abroad at morn
When first the liquid note beloved of men
Comes flying over many a windy wave
To Britain, and in April suddenly
Breaks from a coppice gemm'd with green and red,
And he suspends his converse with a friend,
Or it may be the labour of his hands,
To think or say 'There is the nightingale.'

An answer to the critics on this point has been given by Dr Warren in his comparison of Tennyson and Dante, and I am content to follow the Vice-Chancellor of Oxford and find in the similes of Tennyson the same proportions as in Dante, the same transgression, if such it be, from the main theme to the incidental, the same exorbitant delight

in all the details of the simile. The faults
in the construction and imagination of the
Idylls are great and indefensible, and Sir
Gawain and Sir Tristram have suffered heavy
wrong. But the blame of this is not to be
put upon the Homeric similes. It may be
observed that some of the best and most
elaborate come in the Idyll of *Enid* from
which I have quoted more than once, and
that the story of Enid will stand any fair
test of criticism with regard to its plot, its
characters, its unity of narrative. It is a
poem which atones for a great neglect in
English poetry. Enid, who is more like
Nausicaa than any other earl's daughter of
Romance, had been honoured by all Christen-
dom, except in England, till Tennyson took
up the story from Lady Charlotte Guest's
*Mabinogion* and made good the failure of
the older English minstrelsy. The story in
its older forms, Welsh or French or German
or Norse, is unlike most of the romances; it
is romantic, with not a little of the higher
comedy; romantic without the extravagance

or affectation of the books of chivalry. The
form of *The Lady of Shalott* or *Sir Galahad*
would be quite unfit for this story. It can be
treated in the fullest dramatic way; Geraint
and Enid are modern characters, in every
age that takes any thought about them, in
the nineteenth century with Tennyson as in
the twelfth with Chrestien de Troyes.

Tennyson perhaps never wrote any story
with better success. The form of the dramatic
monologue much more than the narrative
Idyll gave Tennyson what he wanted; for
him as for Browning the dramatic monologue
served better than either narrative or regular
drama. His various imaginative studies are
turned to more profit in this way than in any
other—not only in *Oenone, Ulysses, Tithonus*,
and *Lucretius*, but in *St Simeon Stylites*, and
the *Northern Farmer*, and many more, where
Tennyson plays something like Browning's
game, the humorous sophistry of different
characters making out a case for themselves.
It is in the dramatic Idylls that the intellectual strength of Tennyson is proved,

though some of them may have little value for 'thinkers' in the *Nineteenth Century* meaning of the word. It was not as a 'thinker' of this sort that Tennyson made those early conquests, so well described by so many witnesses, best perhaps by Canon Dixon, as quoted in the *Life of William Morris,* or perhaps in that well-known chapter which describes the perplexities of Colonel Newcome over the taste of the younger generation:—

'He heard opinions that amazed and bewildered him: he heard that Byron was no great poet though a very clever man; he heard that there had been a wicked persecution against Mr Pope's memory and fame, and that it was time to reinstate him; that his favourite Dr Johnson talked admirably, but did not write English; that young Keats was a genius to be estimated in future days with young Raphael, and that a young gentleman of Cambridge, who had lately published two volumes of verses, might take rank with the greatest poets of all.' The friends of

Clive Newcome were probably wiser in their admiration than in their censure, and not unhappy nor unenviable in their praise of 'this young Mr Tennyson of Cambridge.' In spite of the low spirits of Colonel Newcome, these words have a hopeful and cheerful sound about them, in this place especially, and with them I will make an end.

www.ingramcontent.com/pod-product-compliance
Ingram Content Group UK Ltd.
Pitfield, Milton Keynes, MK11 3LW, UK
UKHW042149280225
455719UK00001B/219